Devon Rex Cats

Stephanie Finne

Checkerboard
Library

An Imprint of Abdo Publishing
www.abdopublishing.com

www.abdopublishing.com

Published by Abdo Publishing, a division of ABDO, PO Box 398166, Minneapolis, MN 55439.
Copyright © 2015 by Abdo Consulting Group, Inc. International copyrights reserved in all
countries. No part of this book may be reproduced in any form without written permission from
the publisher. Checkerboard Library™ is a trademark and logo of Abdo Publishing.

Printed in the United States of America, North Mankato, Minnesota.
032014
092014

Cover Photo: Photo by Helmi Flick
Interior Photos: Photos by Helmi Flick pp. 7, 11; iStockphoto pp. 5, 9, 15, 16–17, 17;
    Thinkstock pp. 1, 13, 19, 21

Series Coordinator: Bridget O'Brien
Editors: Tamara L. Britton, Megan M. Gunderson
Art Direction: Renée LaViolette

Library of Congress Cataloging-in-Publication Data

Finne, Stephanie, author.
  Devon Rex cats / Stephanie Finne.
      pages cm -- (Cats. Set II)
  Audience: Ages 8-12.
  Includes index.
  ISBN 978-1-62403-323-0
1. Rex cat--Juvenile literature. 2. Cats--Juvenile literature. I. Title.
  SF449.R4F56 2015
  636.8'2--dc23
                      2013046914

Contents

Lions, Tigers, and Cats

Wild cats have been on Earth for thousands of years. Scientists believe the Miacis was the first ancestor of all cats. This weasel-like animal lived 40 to 50 million years ago!

From this, wild cats adapted to become the animals we know today. Wild cats were known for their hunting abilities. But they were too wild to be kept by humans.

Then about 3,500 years ago, humans began taming cats. These cats were still great hunters. They could help keep pests away from grains and crops. Soon, these **domesticated** cats became companions and beloved pets.

Today, there are more than 40 different cat **breeds**. Whether **domestic** or wild, all cats belong to the family **Felidae**. Some domestic cats look and act like their wild relatives. Others, like the Devon rex, stand out with their **unique** fur and playful personality.

The Devon rex

Devon Rex Cats

Devon rex cats were accepted by the **Cat Fanciers' Association (CFA)** in 1979. However, the first Devon rex was discovered many years before. In 1959, a stray tomcat with a curly coat lived in Buckfastleigh in Devon, England. So did Ms. Beryl Cox.

One day, Ms. Cox adopted a stray female cat with a normal straight **tortie**-and-white coat. Her new pet soon had a **litter** of kittens. A male from the litter was born with a curly coat and pointy ears like the tomcat. Ms. Cox liked the kitten's special looks, funny personality, and loving nature. She named him Kirlee.

Ms. Cox knew about the Cornish rex **breed** discovered ten years before. She felt Kirlee could add to this breed. So, she sold him to a breeder in 1960. Unfortunately, Kirlee had a different type of rex gene.

Breeders called it *Gene II*. Kirlee couldn't be a Cornish rex! He began an entirely new breed of cat, the Devon rex.

In 1967, Devon rex were accepted by a cat registry in the United Kingdom. Finally in 1983, the **CFA** granted the breed championship status.

Devon rexes are nicknamed "poodle cats" because of their curly fur.

Qualities

During its 30-plus years in the **CFA**, the playful Devon rex cat has become a favorite of many owners. These cats quickly learn tricks and will play tag, fetch, and hide-and-seek! They want to be involved in everything. Devon rex cats will wag their tails like dogs and follow their humans everywhere. They are people pleasers, even coming when their name is called.

Owners may talk to their Devon rexes, but these cats are not very talkative. However, they will still make chirping sounds to share something.

Devon rex cats get along well with other pets and children. That's important, because this **breed** does not like being left alone. They are often found on an owner's lap, shoulders, or feet. They eat, sleep, and do chores with their family. If alone for long periods of time, Devon rexes can be destructive.

These cats are elfish in appearance and personality.
They are excellent jumpers. You may find your Devon
rex on top of doors, cupboards,
or appliances! They also love to
be carried or will perch on your
shoulder like a parrot.

Some say Devon
rexes are a cross
between a cat,
a dog, and a
monkey!

Coat and Color

The Devon rex's name reveals something special about its coat. The coat is rexed. Cats with this type of coat have very short guard hairs or none at all. Guard hairs are the long, coarse hairs that protect a cat's undercoat.

The Devon rex **breed** has guard hairs, but there are fewer of them. They also vary in length. This is what gives the coat a lumpy or wavy feeling. The cat's whiskers and eyebrows are also curly. Sometimes, a Devon rex cat only has stubs for whiskers.

The Devon rex has short fur on its back, sides, legs, and tail. The fur is even shorter on the head, ears, neck, chest, and abdomen. Still, the coat is very **dense**. Devon rex cats do **shed**. But their **unique** fur isn't as noticeable.

The coat of a Devon rex comes in any color. It can be solid, shaded, or smoke. It also comes in many patterns, including **tabby**, **bicolor**, **parti-color**, and **pointed**.

All cats have the same body temperature. But Devon rexes often feel warmer than other cats. This is because of their light coat.

Size

The Devon rex cat's **unique** coat covers a well-muscled, medium-sized body. The **breed** has a broad chest and a medium-fine frame. A Devon rex weighs six to nine pounds (3 to 4 kg). Males are heavier than females.

The head of the Devon rex is a modified wedge shape. It features a short **muzzle**, full cheeks, and large, oval eyes. The eyes can be any color.

The Devon rex's ears are large. They sit low on the cat's head. The ears are wide at the base and taper to rounded tips.

The Devon rex's legs are long and slim. The hind legs are longer than the front legs. The back paws have five toes. The front paws have just four toes.

A Devon rex's large ears, upturned nose, and full cheeks give it a unique, elfish appearance.

Care

Devon rex cats need a lot of attention. However, they are easy to care for. They simply require regular checkups with a veterinarian. There, the vet will examine the Devon rex and give it **vaccines**. He or she will also **spay** or **neuter** your pet.

To stay happy and healthy, your Devon rex will also need a few things at home. First, your cat needs to bury its waste. So it will need a **litter box**. Make sure to clean it out every day! Your playful Devon rex will also need lots of toys.

Grooming a Devon rex includes giving it a bath, cleaning its ears, and trimming its claws. A quick wipe down with a damp rag will keep its coat curly.

Finally, you will need to give your Devon rex your time! They love to share your warmth, so be ready to let them on your lap, shoulder, and bed. Including your pet in everything you do will keep it content.

Cats like to scratch. Don't forget to buy your Devon rex a scratching post!

Feeding

Devon rex cats love food as much as they love attention! Be prepared to guard your dinner plate. Still, Devon rex cats will rarely overeat. They will stay a good weight as long as they have a healthy diet.

Your Devon rex cat needs a balanced diet that includes protein. Choose a food that is labeled "complete and balanced." This means your cat will get the **nutrients** it needs.

There are different types of cat food. Canned foods are one option. But, they spoil quickly. Semimoist foods are another option. These foods do not need to be refrigerated. Dry foods help clean your cat's teeth.

Owners also must decide how to feed their cats. Some owners trust their cats with free feeding. In this case, food is always available. Other owners provide food at specific times of day. Still others measure out food, which is called portion fed.

You can discuss feeding options with your vet. No matter how you choose to feed your cat, it is important that it always has fresh water.

Devon rexes will never turn down a meal. Asparagus, cantaloupe, and chicken are some of their favorite people foods.

Kittens

Devon rexes are able to mate when they are between 7 and 12 months old. After mating, a female cat is **pregnant** for about 65 days. She usually gives birth to four kittens in her **litter**.

Kittens are born blind, deaf, and helpless. It takes 10 to 12 days for their senses to develop. They also get teeth during this time. At 3 weeks, they are ready to explore.

For the first 5 weeks, kittens drink their mother's milk. Then, they are **weaned** onto solid food. The kittens spend their time learning and growing. At 12 to 16 weeks old, they are ready for adoption.

Your new Devon rex may not yet have the coat you would expect. Devon rex cats are born with fur. But at 8 weeks old, they **molt**. They will be left with a downy coat on their stomachs that is soft like suede. It can take anywhere from a few days to a year for a new coat to grow. The new coat will have the wavy look of the rexes.

Devon rexes keep their kitten-like personalities as they grow up.

Buying a Kitten

Devon rex cats are active and like a lot of attention. They will live for 20 years. So, be sure you can give a Devon a lot of time for years to come. That's a big responsibility. But Devon rex fans would argue these cats are worth it!

If you decide to get a Devon rex cat, find a reputable **breeder**. Good breeders sell cats that have had **vaccinations**. They know the health and history of their cats. They will be able to find a kitten that is the right fit for your family.

Devon rex cats do **shed** and are not **hypoallergenic**, as some people believe. If you are thinking about getting a Devon rex, be sure to visit it first. It is a good idea to visit it more than once. Wait 24 hours to see if any allergic reactions appear.

If no allergies appear, you are all set to get a Devon rex. Before bringing home your cat, be sure to get some supplies. Provide food and water dishes, food, and a **litter box** to start. You are now ready to welcome your new best friend!

Devon rex cats are loving companions.

Glossary

bicolor - having two colors.

breed - a group of animals sharing the same ancestors and appearance. A breeder is a person who raises animals. Raising animals is often called breeding them.

Cat Fanciers' Association (CFA) - a group that sets the standards for judging all breeds of cats.

dense - thick or compact.

domestic - tame, especially relating to animals.

Felidae (FEHL-uh-dee) - the scientific Latin name for the cat family. Members of this family are called felids. They include lions, tigers, leopards, jaguars, cougars, wildcats, lynx, cheetahs, and domestic cats.

hypoallergenic - unlikely to cause an allergic reaction.

litter - all of the kittens born at one time to a mother cat.

litter box - a box filled with cat litter, which is similar to sand. Cats use litter boxes to bury their waste.

molt - to shed skin, hair, or feathers and replace with new growth.

muzzle - an animal's nose and jaws.

neuter (NOO-tuhr) - to remove a male animal's reproductive glands.

nutrient - a substance found in food and used in the body. It promotes growth, maintenance, and repair.

parti-color - having a dominant color broken up by patches of one or more other colors.

pointed - having color on the head, paws, and tail.

pregnant - having one or more babies growing within the body.

shed - to cast off hair, feathers, skin, or other coverings or parts by a natural process.

spay - to remove a female animal's reproductive organs.

tabby - a coat pattern featuring stripes or splotches of a dark color on a lighter background. Individual hairs are banded with light and dark colors.

tortie (TAWR-tee) - another name for the tortoiseshell pattern, a coat featuring patches of black, orange, and cream.

unique (yoo-NEEK) - being the only one of its kind.

vaccine (vak-SEEN) - a shot given to prevent illness or disease.

wean - to accustom an animal to eating food other than its mother's milk.

Websites

To learn more about Cats,
visit **booklinks.abdopublishing.com**. These links are routinely monitored and updated to provide the most current information available.

Index